The Art of
BRIDGE
BUILDING

◆ FOR THE COMMON CHRISTIAN ◆

Wesley W. Nelson

*Building relationships within the church
and between the church and the world*

Scripture taken from the Holy Bible, New International Version, copyright 1973, 1978, 1984 by the International Bible Publishers. Used by permission of Zondervan Bible Publishers.

ISBN 0-910452-69-5
Copyright © 1989 by Covenant Publications

Design: *David Westerfield*
Production: *Debra J. Almgren, Elsa G. Wiberg, and Jane K. Swanson-Nystrom*

Covenant Publications
3200 West Foster Avenue
Chicago, Illinois 60625
(800) 621-1290, (312) 478-4676

CONTENTS

Preface
5

Is This for Me?
6

CHAPTER ONE
Who and What Are Bridge Builders?
9

CHAPTER TWO
Preparing Ourselves for Bridge Building at All Levels
15

CHAPTER THREE
Level One: Bridge Building in Daily Life
25

CHAPTER FOUR
Level Two: Bridge Building As a Personal Ministry
31

CHAPTER FIVE
Level Three: The Bridge Building Team
43

CHAPTER SIX
The Team Leader
53

The Gentle Army
61

Resources for Sharing the Gospel
62

PREFACE

Rank-and-file Christians generally do very little sharing of God's good news. Most of us waver between guilt over not doing it and short-lived heroic efforts to do it. Those who do it regularly obviously have special gifts. Ought we not expect that God would give us the gifts to do what is so important? Before we attempt to answer this question, we must ask ourselves, "Why did Jesus do it so successfully?" and "How does he want us 'common' Christians to do it?" The answers to these questions lead us to some rather surprising conclusions. There is a way that we can do it, but it is not the way we would expect.

The purpose of this book is to define this revolutionary way of sharing God's good news and to suggest how so-called "common" Christians can do it. The book has been prepared at the request of, and with the cooperation of, the Department of Church Growth and Evangelism. We are grateful to A. Harold and Lorraine Anderson for a grant to assist in its publication.

Wesley W. Nelson
Chicago, Illinois

"IS THIS FOR ME?"

"Bridge builders? I don't know what you're talking about, but if it has to do with communicating anything, I'm sure I couldn't do it. I'm really just a common, ordinary Christian."

"You don't feel qualified to do the things that outstanding Christians do."

"I wish I could be a really effective Christian. I know people who witness whenever they have a chance, but I just can't do it.

"So you feel guilty because you are not the kind of Christian you wish you were, and you can't do anything about it."

"Well, I do feel guilty, in a way, but I'm not a good talker. Oh, I can carry on a conversation, of sorts, but I wouldn't know what to say about religious things, especially to strangers."

"It sounds to me as though you have the qualifications for becoming an excellent bridge builder."

"You're kidding me. I could never do anything like that."

"Do you think you could learn to be a bridge builder?"

"I don't know what you're driving at. I think I'm willing to be taught, but I could never learn to do whatever you're talking about."

"Do you think you could learn to listen to people?"

"Oh, I suppose I could, but you can't communicate anything by listening, can you?"

"Suppose there was a way to communicate that doesn't require you to be a 'good talker,' that works best with so-called 'ordinary' Christians, and that is based on listening and learning. Would that have any appeal to you?"

"Neither of us thinks there is anything like that, but we probably ought to be willing at least to hear about it."

"Fine. You're starting to sound more like a bridge builder. Would you please come with me through this booklet?"

CHAPTER ONE

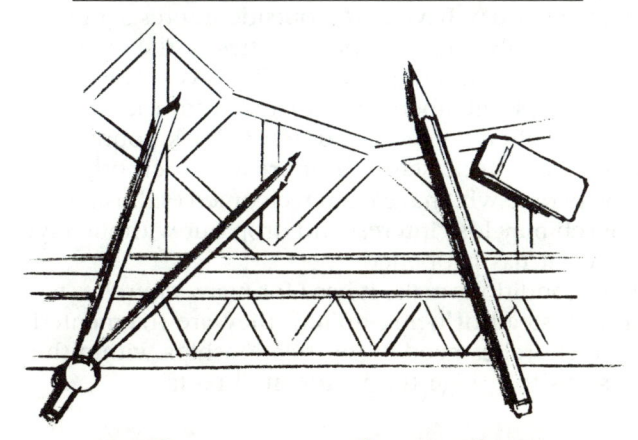

Who and What Are Bridge Builders?

I. BRIDGE BUILDERS ARE PEOPLE WHO BUILD RELATIONSHIPS *between their church and the outside world and within the church itself.*

1) Bridges are needed between the church and the outside world.

Many people have no idea what the church is supposed to be, and they can't see the value of what the church has to offer.

People inside the church can't understand why people outside have so little interest in the church. As a result, many churches are isolated islands in the world.

These churches need closer relationships with the outside world in order to:

    a. help people outside the church appreciate what the church has to offer.

    b. help people of the church have a better understanding of people outside.

2) Bridges are needed within the church itself.

Christians today have many outside interests and generally take part in only a few of the activities of the church. Therefore the church is not the center of their lives. The result is that, in many cases, members are isolated from each other.

Members often come from different backgrounds, and they do not always understand or appreciate each other.

Some people who have been welcomed enthusiastically into the church may lose interest and drop out without anyone realizing what has happened.

These conditions make it hard for many churches to be true families. Instead of being united, they are fragmented.

These churches need closer relationships within their own fellowships to bridge the fragmented parts.

A RESPONSE
☐ "My church needs bridges to the world."
☐ "My church needs bridges within the church itself."
☐ "My church needs both kinds of bridges."

II. BRIDGE BUILDERS MAY WORK AT THREE DIFFERENT LEVELS.

First Level: *Bridge building as a part of daily life*

Those who work at this level do not consider bridge building a special ministry, and they do not schedule special times for it. They build bridges whenever they sense that lines of communication need to be opened during any contacts they may have.

Second Level: *Bridge building as a special personal ministry*

Those individuals or couples who work at this level do so as a special responsibility they have accepted for themselves.

Third Level: *Bridge building as a team ministry*

Those who work at this level serve as members of a bridge building team with regularly scheduled meetings for mutual support, preparation, planning, and reporting.

The same people may work at different levels. The first level is the least demanding, but the third level is the most effective and has the added benefit of working with a support team.

> A RESPONSE
> "I/we wish to engage in bridge building at the following level(s):
>
> ☐ First level   ☐ Third level
> ☐ Second level ☐ Have not decided

III. BRIDGE BUILDERS ARE "COMMON" CHRISTIANS.

In one sense there are no "common" Christians. We are all special in the eyes of God, with unique personalities and different abilities.

In another sense, however, there are common Christians just as there are common people in society. We are common in the sense that we do not occupy prominent positions and that we do not feel comfortable confronting other people concerning decisions they need to make. We are often retiring and sometimes even a bit shy. Since there are a great many of us, it is quite important for us to find ways to serve.

When we hear reports of Christians who easily confront people with the Gospel and who seem to win many people to Christ, we often feel guilty, but we cannot get ourselves to do what they do. We are concerned that we may offend people by saying the wrong thing in the wrong way, and whenever we do make a direct approach in witnessing we feel uncomfortable. We may even say, "I'm just a common Christian. I can't do that." Bridge building is for people who feel this way.

Bridge building is not intended to replace other more direct ministries such as evangelistic visiting, care teams, and visits with the sick and shut-ins. These are primarily directed toward individuals. Bridge builders will also be in contact with individuals, but they will be concerned about relationships between people and how these relationships can affect the welfare of the entire church.

Direct evangelistic visitation is also important, and those who have the gifts for explaining the Gospel to people and inviting them to become Christians should do so. Meanwhile, those who do not have such gifts will be able to engage in bridge building.

Bridge building is different from more direct ministries in the following ways:

1) Our immediate aim as bridge builders will be to make changes in ourselves rather than in other people. We look forward to becoming more mature, more understanding, more caring, and less threatening to others. Any changes in other people will take place as a result of their response to changes in us.

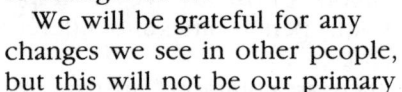

We will be grateful for any changes we see in other people, but this will not be our primary aim, and we will not think of ourselves as failures if we do not see it happening. Bridge building opens doors for closer relationships between people, and we will depend on these closer relationships to produce changes in them. It is quite possible that we will find that we also have gifts for introducing people to Christ or for restoring them to the fellowship of the church. This, however, is not our primary aim, and, again, we will not be disappointed or feel guilty if it does not happen.

In some churches one team may engage in both bridge building and a more direct evangelistic and outreach ministry. When these ministries are combined, the individual team members will use the method for which they feel most suited.

2) Another way in which bridge building is different from more direct ministries is that we, as bridge builders, will take the position of listeners and learners rather than of speakers and teachers. *We discover that more bridge building is done while we listen than while we speak.*

Through listening we learn to know other people as unique individuals, and we learn to care for them. Thus we become more understanding and caring people, and this change in itself often produces changes in other people as they respond to us.

3) A third way in which bridge building differs from more direct ministries is that *we, as bridge builders, do not concern ourselves only with people who have special needs,* such as newcomers, dropouts, lonely or sick people, and unbelievers. Often we discover that those who are ministering to others have many unexpressed hurts and need to know that we care, while those who appear to be in need are really quite comfortable.

> FOR INSTANCE
> Have you ever thought about how many hurts a busy church leader may have? This person, who serves others, may be the one who needs our encouragement. On the other hand, a person who is not involved in anything might be helped most by an opportunity to serve.

Listening and learning are most effective when we are in touch with a variety of people. As we listen to and learn from them, we develop a broad understanding of a cross section of people—of what hurts them and how they receive comfort, of what they have to give to us, and of the satisfaction they receive from giving.

> SUMMARY
> The differences between bridge building and more direct ministries are:
> 1) The immediate aim of bridge builders is to make changes in themselves rather than in other people. Changes in other people often come when they respond to changes in the bridge builders.
> 2) Bridge builders take the lower place of listeners and learners and are concerned about what other people have to offer them as well as what they have to offer other people.
> 3) Bridge builders make contacts with a cross section of people, not just with those who seem to have needs.

> **CHAPTER SUMMARY**
> 1) Bridge builders are people who build relationships between their church and the world and within their church itself.
> 2) Bridge builders may work at three levels.
> 3) Bridge builders are common Christians who feel more comfortable serving in this way than in a more direct ministry.

In the next chapter we turn our attention to preparing ourselves for bridge building at all levels.

CHAPTER TWO

Preparing Ourselves for Bridge Building at all Levels

MAKING CHANGES IN OURSELVES RATHER THAN IN OTHERS?

In the previous chapter we stated that the immediate aim of bridge builders is to make changes in ourselves rather than in others. Why should we think about making changes ourselves when the people we are contacting are obviously the ones who need changing? They need help; they need to become Christians; they need to be brought back into church; they need to have their relationship with Christ restored. Why should we be the ones to change?

THE EXAMPLE OF JESUS

Jesus is the great bridge builder. He built a bridge between heaven and earth to reconcile us to God. He built a bridge between people to reconcile us to each other.

In order to become the great bridge builder, Jesus began by making changes himself. He left heaven and came to earth to live among us. Though he was equal with God, he "made himself nothing," and became one of us. He even took the lowest place among us when he died on the cross for us.

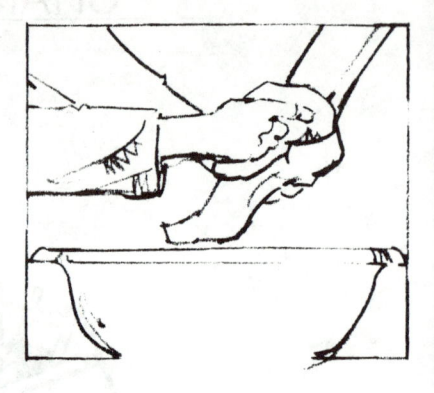

If we expect to be effective bridge builders our attitude should be the same as his:

> Your attitude should be the same as that of Christ Jesus: Who, being in very nature God, did not consider equality with God something to be grasped, but made himself nothing, taking the very nature of a servant, being made in human likeness. And being found in appearance as a man, he humbled himself . . ." (Philippians 2:5-8).

We begin building bridges to other people by assuming this attitude of humility.

OTHERS CHANGE IN RESPONSE TO CHANGES IN US.

When we became reconciled to God by believing in Jesus, we were responding to what he did when he left the place of highest authority to take the lowest place on the cross.

In a similar way, other people can be influenced to change only as they respond to changes they see in us. Obviously we cannot do what Jesus did, but we are expected to have the same attitude of humility. If Jesus found it necessary to humble himself in order to build bridges, we must also assume this attitude of humility in order to build bridges.

WE BUILD BRIDGES BY TAKING THE LOWER PLACE.

When we come to people to try to get them back to church or believe in Jesus, we may appear condescending. After all, we go to church and they do not, or we are believers and they are not. In their minds, this puts us in the upper place and them in the lower place. As a result we become a threat to them, and they erect a barrier.

On the other hand, if we come to people to listen and to learn to know them better, we are no longer a threat and we open the way for bridge building.

WE BECOME LEARNERS AND LISTENERS.

Since the learner has a lower place than the teacher, we humble ourselves by taking the learner's place. By becoming listeners we show that we are interested in what they have to say, and thus we pay respect to them and give them the upper place.

We ask ourselves: *"What can I learn from contact with this person?"* rather than, "What can I teach this person?" and *"What can I hear from this person?"* rather than, "What can I say to this person?"

LEARNING TO LISTEN

Listening does not come easily for most of us; we generally find it easier to talk. Therefore we must practice listening until it becomes natural.

More bridge building is done while we are listening than while we are talking.

OBJECTION
I enjoy talking. Does this mean that I must listen all the time and never get to talk?

ANSWERS
1) By no means. It would not be a conversation if you did not participate. Just be sure the other person wants to hear you and is not just being courteous. Refrain from long monologues and stories that get boring, and be sure the person to whom you are building a bridge is encouraged to say anything he or she wishes to say. Remember: *We do most of our bridge building while the other person is speaking.*

2) Many of us enjoy talking more than listening. Therefore we need times when we may indulge ourselves without restriction. Sometimes we need to pour out our troubles to a trusted friend, and at other times we need to sit around a dinner table trading stories. We may discover, of course, as we learn some of the pleasures of listening, that even here we enjoy listening more and more. Meanwhile there is no reason to deny ourselves the luxury of unrestricted talk fests from time to time. At these times go ahead and talk. Who knows, maybe one of your friends is trying to build a bridge to you!

LOVE IS OUR AIM.

In our listening and learning, love is our final aim. As we hear and learn from other people, we come to understand them better, and God puts love in our hearts for them.

The Bible teaches us to "follow the way of love" (1 Corinthians 14:1). Therefore, our aim must always be to love the people to whom we are trying to build bridges.

When people discover that we really love them, they sense that we are bridging a gap between us and them, and relationships begin to be built.

Most of us, however, do not love other people as Jesus did. We are often motivated by guilt or by what people may think of us. People have learned to be suspicious of those who claim to love them. The fact that our love is so often inadequate gives people reason to be suspicious of us also. They responded when Jesus spoke to them, not only because he had humbled himself, but also because he really loved them. As we humble ourselves and take the lower place by listening to people and learning from them, our love also grows more real. When people sense this happening to us, it becomes much more natural for them to respond.

SOME INADEQUATE FORMS OF LOVE

1) Superficial "love"

Commercial enterprises often use the word "love" superficially. "We love our customers," they say. While it is legitimate for business personnel to express love for their customers, people generally suspect that their greatest concern is the success of their business. People tend to have the same suspicions about the church. They suspect that the church thinks of them as "prospects" or "customers" and that Christians claim to love them in order to spread their own religious views or to get them to come to their church.

Therefore, to emphasize the unique nature of Christian love, we must lay aside our concerns for the welfare of our church and even our concern for spreading our faith. Our first step must always be to learn to love people regardless of their response. Once we learn to love, we will be able to decide what the next step will be.

2) Sentimental "love"

Sometimes we become more concerned about being known as loving people than about love itself. When this happens we force our love on people whether they want it or not. We may have such a need to be loving that we commit ourselves beyond what God expects of us and become distressed by guilt.

In other cases we may be threatened by people who demand more than we are prepared to give. Then we may try to outdo ourselves in order to prove to them that we really do love them. To avoid this threat, we must prayerfully evaluate the energy and the time we have available, and refrain from exceeding these limits. *We, not others, must be the ones to determine how much love we will give.*

3) Token "love"

In our efforts to be loving, we may be tempted to concentrate on one or two individuals to whom we can then point as shining examples of what happens when we love. We need to remember that there are many other people who also need our love. As bridge builders, we seek to strike a balance between concentrating on a few and being available to many.

THE NATURE OF REAL LOVE

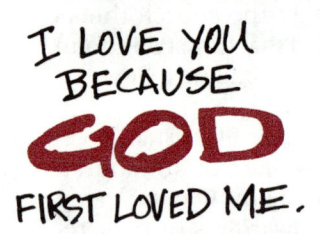

Real love comes only from God. It is the love we are able to give because God first loved us (see 1 John 4:16-19). Therefore, *we concentrate on God's love for us and love people only to the extent that God's love makes it normal for us to do so.* To do more than this will cause bridge building to become burdensome, and we may soon burn out.

Since we expect to be concerned about a number of people, we do not expend our resources on loving in depth. We try to refer people who desire in-depth loving to someone who can assess their needs and give them the attention they require.

AN OBJECTION

I really don't have very much real love. I'm afraid the love I do have is of the inadequate kind. Does this mean that I cannot be a bridge builder?

ANSWER

By no means. It just means that you are like most of us. At this point sincerity is more important than a profession of great love.

We begin by simply recognizing that we do not love other people very much. We do not make any claims of being loving people. Instead, we think of ourselves as "learning to love."

Meanwhile, Jesus Christ, the great bridge builder, has promised to be with us. "Surely I will be with you always," he said (Matthew 28:20).

Every time we make a contact, it is Jesus making that contact. Every time we make a phone call, it is Jesus speaking through us. Every time we enter a home, Jesus enters that home and wants to make his presence felt.

So relax. Bridge building is an exercise in simply trusting God and depending on the Holy Spirit. Step out in faith and see what the Lord will do through you, a common Christian!

LEARNING TO LOVE

Since the Bible tells us to "follow the way of love" (1 Corinthians 14:1), it must be possible to learn to love.

As long as people are just "people" to us, we cannot love them. As we begin to know certain people as unique individuals, we find it possible to learn to love them. God's gift of love comes to us as we begin to understand their interests and ambitions, their joys and disappointments, their temptations and hurts—as we begin to understand the reasons why they are as they are. We learn these things through listening. Therefore, *we learn to love through listening.*

> **TWO QUESTIONS**
> 1) Do you see yourself as a loving person?
> 2) Are you willing to try to learn to love?

If you can more easily answer yes to the second question, you are much more likely to become a good bridge builder.

LOVE ITSELF WILL LEAD US TO THE NEXT STEP.

What happens next? At this point we don't have to know the answer to this question. Once we have learned to love another person sincerely, though only a little, love will guide us to the next step.

Our responsibility is to come to the place where we are motivated by love. Then the Holy Spirit, who is the Spirit of love, will show us what to do next.

AT WHAT LEVEL DO YOU EXPECT TO BUILD BRIDGES?

What happens next will depend to some extent on what level you expect to serve as a bridge builder. In the next chapter we consider some possibilities for building bridges as a part of daily living (first level).

BASIC PRINCIPLES TO REMEMBER

The two basic principles to remember in all levels of bridge building are:

1) Our immediate concern is changing ourselves.

In this we follow the example of Jesus, who humbled himself and took the lower place. We humble ourselves by becoming listeners and learners. The test of our success as bridge builders is whether we are becoming more caring. Bridges are built as people respond to what happens to us.

2) Our immediate aim is to learn to love.

We do not profess to have much love, but we are learners, learning to love. We seek to get beyond inadequate forms of love to the true love that comes only from God. As we listen and learn, we begin to understand other people better, and as God gives us the gift of real love, we learn to love them more. As other people sense that we are really beginning to love them, the barriers are broken, and bridges are built. When we have learned to love, even a little, love will lead us to the next step.

> SUMMARY
> As we begin bridge building, we remember two principles:
> 1) Our immediate concern is to see changes in ourselves.
> 2) Our immediate aim is to learn to love.

CHAPTER THREE

Level One: Bridge Building in Daily Life

> REVIEW
> Before proceeding farther, let us review what we mean by bridge building. We Christians are often isolated from people outside the church and even from each other. We do not understand each other or care for each other as we might. Bridge building is an effort to bring people together to help them get to know and care for each other more. In bridge building we concentrate first of all on ourselves. By following Jesus' example we assume an attitude of humility, and we learn to respect other people. This paves the way for better understanding and more care. This first level offers many opportunities for bridge building even though the second and third levels generally bring us into closer relationships.

This chapter is for people who wish to build bridges in their daily relationships. It also has value for those who plan to go on to practice bridge building as a special ministry.

TWO VISITORS

Some time ago a man rang my doorbell. From his visit, together with the one that followed a few days later, I learned some lessons about bridge building in daily life. When I answered my doorbell, the man at the door immediately began talking. "Good morning, Mr. Nellson," he said. "How glad I am to see you."

"Yes?" I responded cautiously, waiting for him to begin his pitch. I was sure he had not rung my doorbell just to tell me how glad he was to see me.

"Mr. Nelson," he continued, "I have something that can change your whole life."

"What is it?" I asked. It turned out to be a publication for which he was selling subscriptions. I was not interested in the publication, and I failed to see how it could change my life. The more he talked the less interested I became, and finally I brought the visit to a conclusion as kindly as I could. It is possible that he really did have a publication that would change my life. If so, we both failed. I failed to obtain it, and he failed in the purpose for which he came to my door.

Days later the doorbell rang again, and I heard another man saying, "Good morning, Mr. Nelson. How glad I am to see you."

"Oh, no," I said to myself, "Not this again!" But this man went on to say that he had heard me preach when he was a high-school student and that I had helped him. "I decided to stop by while I was in town to thank you," he said. "I feel that I would like to get to know you a little better."

I was still suspicious and asked him a few more questions, but before long I opened the screen door and invited him in.

He had little more to say about himself after he was seated in my living room. Instead, he continued to show an interest in me and in my welfare. I had a problem that was not particularly confidential but that had caused me considerable anxiety. Before I realized what I was doing, I found myself telling him about the problem. In this way we spent what to me was a delightful hour over a cola and some cookies.

After he left, I felt as though I had made a real friend. I wondered why I had shared my concern with him. I realized that I had done most of the talking and that he seemed to be listening most of the time. What impressed me most was that it was really true, as he had said, that he wanted to get to know me a little better. He had accomplished his purpose, and I felt as though I had gained something by his visit.

LESSONS FOR BRIDGE BUILDING

From the viewpoint of bridge building, the first visitor was at a disadvantage. He was trying to sell me something I did not need, which is not conducive to the best relationship, and his time was severely limited. It is a mistake, however, to assume that a perfect situation and much time are always required for bridge building.

AN EXAMPLE

I was staying in a hotel far from home, and I was suffering from cataracts. I stumbled as I entered the elevator and mumbled to another passenger about my impaired sight. He gave me his full attention all the way down to the first floor, and then as he stepped out of the elevator, he said, "They're doing wonderful things for that kind of problem now." The words he spoke weren't great in themselves, but the attention he gave me, the way he listened to me, and the sincerity with which he spoke turned my whole attitude around. He had diverted his attention from his own interests to listen to me and respond, and I responded to him. The bridge was built in the elevator between the fourth and the first floor. There had been no time for preparation, and there could be no follow-up, but in this case none was needed. The bridge served its own purpose.

Obviously we cannot think about bridge building when we are as busy as the magazine salesperson. However, the resources of our Christian faith make it possible to assume an underlying attitude of humility and a desire to learn to love people. Then, when opportunities for bridge building come, we will be able to respond spontaneously.

The situation of the second visitor was much more suited to bridge building. Though he probably had no intention of building bridges, he did it spontaneously.

He took the lower place of the listener, and he did not come to make any change in me. Yet I responded to what had happened to him, and my life was enriched by his coming.

If he had come to persuade me to visit his church, I probably would not have responded. However, if he had come as he did, to thank me and affirm me, and if he had listened as he did, he would have built a loving relationship. This relationship would serve as a bridge over which I might well have come to his church.

BEGINNING THE PRACTICE OF BRIDGE BUILDING

As you begin practicing bridge building in your daily contacts, you will find opportunities from time to time. Following are some that will come naturally:

• At a chance meeting on a street corner or in a grocery store.

• During a visit with a friend after church or after a club meeting.

• In a conversation with someone during an informal social gathering.

• During a luncheon or coffee date with an acquaintance.

• During a visit with a stranger on a bus or train or plane.

• During a telephone conversation with a friend or acquaintance.

Following are some more difficult situations:

- During the brief contacts with your waitress or waiter in a restaurant.

- When your mail carrier or delivery person comes to your door.

- When a representative of a cult or another religion comes to your door.

- When someone dials the wrong number and gets you by mistake.

SOME SUGGESTIONS AND CAUTIONS

- Bridge building is a spiritual service. We are able to love only because God first loved us. Therefore prayer and dependence on the Holy Spirit are extremely important.

- Seek sincerity. Be aware of the nature of true love and try to get beyond the inadequate forms of love described in chapter two (See pages 19-20).

- Always remember to show an interest the next time you meet someone who has previously expressed some concern to you. To neglect to do this is to signal that you really do not care.

- Avoid the temptation to be excessively enthusiastic, condescending, or frivolous. If time allows only a brief conversation, make it positive, encouraging, and genuine. Be sure to be responsive and sympathetic to the mood of the other person.

- Find ways to refer people to others who ask for more attention than you are able to give them. To refer people to other caring people is in itself an act of bridge building. Learn to differentiate between those who can be helped by further attention and those who become increasingly dependent. If you need guidance at this point, talk with your pastor or another qualified person.

- Evaluate yourself after every experience of bridge building. What happened to you? Did you really take the lower place by being a listener and a learner? Did you learn to understand and care a little (or a little more) for this person?

> **RESULTS TO EXPECT**
> 1) You will become more caring and more interested in the welfare of other people.
> 2) People will come to you with problems and concerns. They will almost always want someone who will listen and show an interest in them. Rarely will they want advice even if they seem to be asking for it.
> 3) You may have opportunities to introduce people to Jesus as Savior and Lord. Do not be troubled if you do not feel qualified to do this. You have three alternatives from which to choose:
>   a. Arrange for a qualified and gifted person to meet with them. This is a legitimate act of bridge building.
>   b. Give them a suitable tract, like the one attached to the center of this booklet or one of the tracts listed at the end.
>   c. Do it yourself, using a suitable tract to guide you if you wish.
>
> No one of these is the best alternative. Choose the one with which you feel most comfortable.

In the next chapter you will find ten guidelines that are especially important for bridge building as a special ministry. They are also valuable for those who wish to practice it in their daily lives but do not plan to make a special ministry of it.

Now, as you begin practicing bridge building, may God make this a rewarding and fulfilling part of your life.

CHAPTER FOUR

Level Two: Bridge Building as a Personal Ministry

Some of you who read this manual will want to commit yourselves to bridge building as a special ministry, either alone or together with your spouse or a close friend, and either on your own or as part of a church ministry.

YOUR COMMITMENT

The effectiveness of this ministry will depend on your commitment and how faithfully you keep it. The commitment should not be so light that it requires no sacrifice, but it should not be so heavy that it wears on you.

For instance, you might commit yourself to one period of intentional bridge building per week for one year. This might include hospitality in your home, visits in other homes, a couple of hours spent on the telephone, or any other method you might devise. Make a reasonable commitment, allow for occasional interruptions, and then determine to keep it faithfully and give it priority over other responsibilities.

REMEMBERING YOUR PERSPECTIVE

It is important to keep your perspective constantly before you to help you remember what your aims and goals are. The unique features of bridge building, as summarized on page 14, are:

1) Your immediate aim will be to make changes in yourself—to become more understanding of other people and to become more caring. Changes in other people will come as they see what happens to you. Meanwhile, as you learn to love other people, love will guide you to your next step.

2) You will follow Jesus' example of humility and take the lower place by becoming a listener and a learner. As such you will not be a threat to other people, and they will feel free to respond to you.

3) You will make contacts with a broad cross section of people, not just with those who have needs. This cross section of contacts will give you a better understanding of people and will help you find ways of bridging the gaps between them as you learn to love them.

DEFINING YOUR FIELD OF SERVICE

In order to prepare for the third feature listed above, you will need to define your field as broadly as possible. This may be done by preparing several lists in categories like those listed below. The "a" and "b" parts of each category will generally represent the extremes in that category, and the lists will represent as wide a field of your acquaintances and your church family as possible.

1) a. Regular attenders of the church whom you would like to get to know better
   b. Dropouts and inactive members who rarely, if ever, attend

2) a. Older people, beyond retirement age
   b. Young people of high school age

3) a. People who have been members for many years
   b. Newcomers who have just joined or who have not yet joined

4) a. Faithful and hardworking Sunday school teachers, youth leaders, members of church boards, and officers of the church
   b. People who attend with some regularity but who assume no further responsibilities

5) a. Pastoral staff and their families
   b. Parents of children and young people who come to Sunday school or youth activities but who never attend church themselves

6) a. People who have recently visited your church for the first time
   b. Friends or neighbors who have little or no contact with a church

These lists will represent the different kinds of people to whom and between whom you might expect to build bridges.

Keep the lists for future use in bridge building. Undoubtedly you will revise and add to them and discover other categories. In your work of bridge building, you will probably never cover all the people on your lists. Many of these people may seem too threatening for you to try to contact. Keep them on the list anyway. Someday you might feel differently about them. What is important is that these lists contain as wide a variety of people as possible.

TEN GUIDELINES FOR BRIDGE BUILDING

The guidelines that follow are not to be memorized. Instead, notice how natural and practical they are, and become so familiar with their emphasis that you use them without thinking. To illustrate how these guidelines work in actual experience, they are included in examples of conversations with different people.

There is nothing sacred about these guidelines. They should be tested in your own practice of bridge building and revised to fit your own needs.

I. A CONVERSATION *with a woman who, with her children, has just visited our church for the first time*

The bridge builder begins:
"I'm from First Church. We were happy to have you visit our church last Sunday. Have you just moved to town?"
"Yes."
"Where did you come from?"
"Atlanta."
"What does your husband do?"
"My husband is an electrical engineer by trade, but he lost his job, and now he's just working as a handyman, and he hates it."

GUIDELINE 1: DON'T BE AN INTERROGATOR

"That reminds me of the time I lost my job and had to take anything I could get for several months, and I know how terrible I felt. We didn't have enough to eat for a while. Believe me, I know how you must feel. By the way, how many children do you have?"
"We have three."
"Boys or girls?"
"Two boys and one girl."
"And what ages are they?"
(And thus the conversation continued.)

This budding bridge builder wanted to get to know this family so he did the obvious thing, he asked a lot of questions. How else could he get to know them?

GUIDELINE 2: Don't Interrupt

Yet with all his questioning, he was not building any bridges. He was getting to know *about* this woman's family, but he was not getting really to know *her*.

He was not even getting to know *about* her—whether she worked outside the home or whether, in fact, she was a single mother. By directing the conversation so quickly to her husband, he was saying that he was not really interested in her. We are supposed to be humbling ourselves and taking the lower place, but, by dominating the conversation with questions, this bridge builder was really taking the upper place.

This woman may have wanted to express some other concerns. The bridge builder should have given her an opportunity to do this by pausing a few moments and then showing an interest in any concerns she may have had.

GUIDELINE 3: Don't Change the Subject

One of these questions may have led into a conversation if the bridge builder had not kept changing the subject with another question. Remember, *bridges are built by what you hear the other person say*. As you listen, you are beginning to care for this person and a bridge is being built.

It often takes a little while for people to gather their thoughts and say what they would like. Sometimes they don't quite know what to say or how to say it.

GUIDELINE 4: Don't Be Afraid of Silence

35

If we become embarrassed by silence, we try to make conversation, and this robs the other person of the opportunity to say what he or she would like to talk about. It takes experience to learn how long to wait before making a comment. However, most of us are guilty of speaking too soon or too much.

This bridge builder should have been alert to the feelings the woman expressed about her husband's loss of his job. Sometimes feelings like these are not rational, and there is no point in getting into a discussion about them or to suggest that the other person should not have these feelings. The important thing is to try to understand how the other person feels, even if it may not make sense to you.

GUIDELINE 5: LISTEN FOR DEEP FEELINGS

GUIDELINE 6: "TELL ME MORE" IS BETTER THAN, "THAT REMINDS ME"

Another mistake this bridge builder made was to refer to his own experience at this sensitive moment. Phrases like, "That reminds me," should generally be avoided in building bridges. A better response is something like, "Tell me more."

Let's try an imaginary conversation again and see if we can build a bridge to this woman:

"I'm from First Church. We were happy to have you visit our church last Sunday. I understand that you have just moved to town."

"Yes."

We do not respond immediately in case the woman wishes to say something more. If she says nothing further, we might say: "Moving is sometimes difficult. I wonder how it was for you."

"Oh, it was terrible. We had close friends where we came from. Even the children had a lot of friends, and my husband enjoyed his work so much—until he lost his job."

"So right now you are a bit discouraged."

"Well, not really. Our new neighbors have been very nice to us, but they can't take the place of old friends. I was on the phone for an hour last night with one of our neighbors back in Atlanta."

"And your husband is not enjoying his new job as much as his last one."

"No, not at all. He had to take this job as a handyman, and he just hates it."

"This must make it hard for him."

"Yes. I keep trying to tell him it's just temporary—until he can find something in his own profession."

In this conversation, this woman has much more freedom to tell us whatever she wishes. Her natural responses give us an opportunity to learn to know her as a unique person and to identify with her. With this comes a sense of real caring for her and her family.

We hope that we will be able to be of some help to her and her family, but our immediate goal is to get to know her as a unique individual so we may learn to care for her. After we have learned to care, we can decide what the next step should be.

II. A BRIDGE BUILDING CONVERSATION
with a critical person

During the conversation, this person says:

"I must confess that I don't care at all for your pastor's preaching."

Some answers might be:

"Last Sunday's sermon may not have been the pastor's best. Why don't you give the pastor another chance?"

"Preaching isn't the pastor's greatest gift, but there are so many other gifts that they make up for poor preaching."

"The pastor is sincere, which is more than we can say of some ministers. I feel that sincerity is what really counts."

"You have to admit that the pastor really did preach God's Word."

All of these responses are defensive, and they do not build any bridges. A better response might be:

"From what you say, I realize that you appreciate good preaching."

Perhaps you can think of an even better response. Use one that will get the conversation off the criticism and on the person and try to keep the conversation positive.

While building bridges you need not defend your church or pastor or even your own views.

Try to understand the critic's viewpoint. With understanding comes caring, and your aim—to learn to care—has been fulfilled.

GUIDELINE 7: REFRAIN FROM BEING DEFENSIVE

You may feel that this person is too critical ever to feel happy in your church. You may not even wish to continue the relationship. You need never feel under any compulsion to do this, but the Holy Spirit may lead you to develop such a true caring relationship that you will be able to help this person to become less critical.

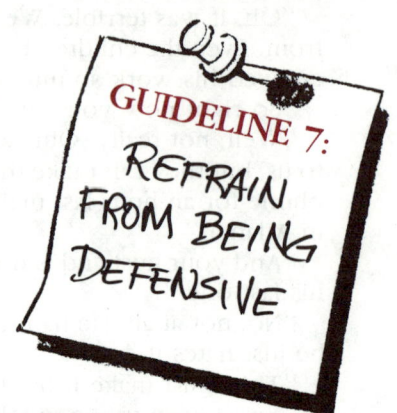

GUIDELINE 8: YOU CAN SAY ALMOST ANYTHING TO A PERSON WHO KNOWS YOU REALLY CARE

In trying to avoid being defensive, you may swing to the other extreme and become critical yourself. Allow the critic to speak, and try to understand his or her reasoning, but do not join in the criticism or become critical yourself.

GUIDELINE 9: DON'T BECOME CRITICAL

III. A BRIDGE BUILDING CONVERSATION
with a member who has dropped out of church

After some light conversation, this person says: "I know I haven't been in church for a long time. I have been awfully busy, but I should be getting back now soon."

Some responses might be:
"We have missed you and will be glad to see you again."
"Would you mind telling us why you dropped out?"
"It really is your Christian responsibility to attend church regularly."

These are all patronizing responses. They put us in the upper instead of the lower place. A better response would be something like:
"I really came to visit because I don't know you very well and I'd like to get better acquainted."

In order to make this response honestly, we must give attention to our own attitude. We must not think of people as "dropouts" or "unbelievers." Instead, we think of them as people we need to get to know better so we can learn to care for them.

GUIDELINE 10: OUR AIM IN BRIDGE BUILDING IS TO GET TO KNOW PEOPLE AS UNIQUE PERSONS SO WE MAY LEARN TO LOVE THEM

Getting to know people so we may learn to love them involves an entire change in attitude for many of us. We will be contacting people from the most active to the least interested, from firm believers to confirmed unbelievers, but to us they will merely be people for whom we want to learn to care.

SUMMARY

Ten guidelines for bridge building:
1) Don't be an interrogator.
2) Don't interrupt.
3) Don't change the subject.
4) Don't be afraid of silence.
5) Listen for deep feelings.
6) "Tell me more" is better than "That reminds me."
7) Refrain from being defensive.
8) You can say almost anything to a person who knows you really care.
9) Don't become critical.
10) Our aim in bridge building is to get to know people as unique individuals so we may learn to love them.

Can you give illustrations of the ten guidelines from any recent conversations that you have had?

Listen to the conversation when you are part of a group. Are the participants showing each other respect by listening? Is the conversation bringing them together? Is any bridge building going on?

Bridge building can be a fulfilling personal ministry for you.

As you become a more caring and more understanding person, people will respond and their lives will also be changed. As you serve in this way, you may come to realize how much more fulfilling it could be if you were part of a bridge building team. Perhaps you might even become the leader. For further information, turn to the next chapters.

CHAPTER FIVE

Level Three: The Bridge Building Team

OBSERVING A TEAM MEETING

We arrive a few minutes before 9:30 on a Sunday morning. The team meets during the Sunday-school hour. Team members find it too taxing to have Sunday-school responsibilities in addition to this service, so their meeting becomes their Sunday-school class.

> Though this is a bridge building team, this group prefers to use the name "Ambassadors." Names like ministers of care, or lay associate pastors might also be used.

By 9:30 three members and two guests have arrived and are chatting together. Three members have not yet arrived. The team leader says, "Mary, you mentioned last week that you were having a problem on your job. Are things going better now?"

Mary tells how things are going, and the group responds to

her problem. Then the leader turns to Bill, "I understand you were discouraged about your visit last week. Will you tell us about it?"

Bill describes a visit with a particularly noncommunicative person. He feels that the visit had been a total loss. The matter is discussed briefly, some members share similar experiences. Bill discovers that he has learned something from the visit and from the discussion. Since being a "learner" was the purpose of the visit, it was a success, and he feels encouraged.

The leader has kept the discussion well in hand and makes sure it does not drag on too long. It is now less than ten minutes after starting time. Much has been accomplished, and the three late comers have arrived.

We hardly notice that the meeting has started. The group has kept on chatting—under the direction of the leader. How much better this seems to us than to say, "It's time to begin. Let's start with prayer." We also notice that the meeting has started on time, even though three members were missing.

Other concerns are shared, and there is a brief time of prayer during which these concerns are remembered.

We learn that there are six team members. Four others attend the meeting as guests. One of the ministries of the team is to invite guests to attend as many sessions as they like. Two of these guests are new members of the church. The other two are church members who have never really become a part of the church family. They have responded to the invitations of two of the team members to visit their meetings because they sense that the team members really care for them. The host team members make sure their guests are made to feel at home in the meeting.

In some churches the team may be larger, and in others it may be smaller. As few as two or three people might form a team. Inviting guests to the meetings is important to the bridge building ministry. In some cases there might be more guests than team members.

The team members model, in the meeting, what they will be doing in their weekly assignments. They are learning to care for each other and their guests, and they prac-

tice listening to each other and learning from each other. Team members are always free to invite people they contact to be guests at the meetings. In this way more people are exposed to the loving family spirit that is at the heart of the church.

After the prayer, a problem is considered. The team members are having difficulty contacting people. They propose that instead of phoning to make appointments, occasionally they will do their visiting while they are on the phone. In some cases, they will drop in unannounced with a gift for a child or an item of food or a piece of interesting literature, and they will not even try to get into the house. While these suggestions have value and may be used in some cases, the team members agree to concentrate on those people with whom they already have some contact and who will likely welcome them.

The two new church members who are guests urge the team members not to be discouraged. They themselves had not been very responsive, but they had been won over by people who really cared for them.

Versatility is one of the marks of this team ministry. It is not bound to any specific "program." If one method is not effective, another will be tried.

The team keeps in mind that the successful method is the one that is helping them develop a more understanding and caring attitude. If they are learning to care, they will be building bridges to people even though they may not see themselves as being successful.

> THE TEAM MEETING: AN ABSOLUTE NECESSITY
> 1) For mutual care and support.
> 2) To model the principles of humility and learning to love.
> 3) To keep adjusting the ministry to meet changing situations.
> 4) To remind one another of the aims and purposes of bridge building.
> 5) To expose visitors to a loving fellowship.
> 6) To recruit potential team members from among the visitors.
>
> In many cases more bridge building may go on in the meeting than in the weekly assignments. This is one reason why bridge building should not be called a visitation ministry. Visiting may be only a small part of bridge building.

The real genius of this ministry is the combination of its meetings and its mission, as illustrated in the following: the team members gather weekly to refresh their spirits and restore their resources; then they scatter to fulfill at least one act of service before they gather again.

This pattern was established by Jesus himself. He said that his followers would "come in and go out, and find pasture" (John 10:9). "Coming in" to be refreshed and "going out" to serve are equally important. Going out repeatedly without coming in leads to burn out. Those who go out need also to come in for the refreshing resources of fellowship with others who are engaged in similar tasks.

If the meetings are not balanced with a mission, however, the participants become ingrown and preoccupied with their own needs. Jesus has promised to be with them when they are gathered for refreshing, but he has also promised to be with them as they scatter to fulfill their mission. They need to learn to trust him to be with them as they go out to serve him as well as when they are in their meetings.

GIVING OUT ASSIGNMENTS

The team members usually give reports on their assignments for the week. Not everyone reports each week, and the reports generally include only the points of special interest to the group. At some meetings, one report may be so significant that all the available time is spent on that report. Other reports may be held over until the next week. At this meeting, so much time has been spent in discussing a problem that no reports are given.

The leader now makes sure that each team member has several assignments. By having several, the members will be more sure to contact at least one. No more than one contact will be expected from each team member per week.

Some time is spent discussing the assignments, and team members decide whether to go alone or in pairs. Team members who do not have cars pair up with those who do. The individuals or pairs determine whether they should make a visit in a home, arrange a luncheon or coffee date, invite their assigned person to their own home, or make contact some other way.

The guests are invited to pair up with someone if they wish. In these cases contacts will usually be made with active church members, who can help assimilate these people into the church family.

The meeting ends with this informal planning of how to fulfill the assignments.

KEEPING RECORDS

Assignments will normally be made from lists like those suggested on page 33, together with names that come immediately to the minds of team members. These lists should, of course, be updated continually, especially to include people who have recently visited the church or who have become new members.

A simple record system such as the one suggested below may be used. If desired, cards of different colors may be used to designate different categories in the lists. If your church is small, you may not even need a system like the one suggested. However, it is surprising how quickly a list will grow, and there is value in going through the cards from time to time to make sure that no one is being lost.

A SIMPLE RECORD SYSTEM
- Put names, addresses, and phone numbers on cards.
- Make duplicate cards, one white, the other any other color.
- White card: given to bridge builder(s) to whom the assignment is made.
- Colored card: kept by the leader, who writes on it the name(s) of the bridge builder(s) assigned to make the contact.
- White card: returned by bridge builder(s) after contact has been made, with date of contact, brief report and name(s) of bridge builder(s) who made the contact. This information is later transferred by leader or record keeper to colored card.
- If possible, give each bridge builder or pair several assignments even though no more than one assignment will be expected to be completed each week.

FORMATION OF THE TEAM

The team may come into being in a number of ways, such as:

1) A group already in existence may be requested to become a bridge building team.

2) Some members of the diaconate or other boards may be asked to become the core of such a group.

3) People may be recruited and formed into a team by one or two individuals who are already involved in bridge building.

CONTINUOUS RECRUITING

Since the greatest benefits come to the team members themselves, there is value in having as many team members as are available, up to the point at which the group becomes too large. The entire church would benefit if most of the members would give some time to this team.

Therefore recruiting may go on continually. Recruits may come from bridge building contacts you have made. Remember that this is a place for common Christians. They need not be special. Invite them to be guests at a few meetings. Then invite them to pair with team members for a few contacts. If they are willing to make a commitment to this ministry, invite them to become members of the team.

COMMITMENT TO THE TEAM

A reasonable commitment to this ministry might be:

1) To attend the weekly team meetings regularly.

2) To complete one bridge building assignment each week.

3) To make these commitments for a period of one year.

These commitments are similar to those of choir members or Sunday-school teachers, who are expected to serve on Sundays and spend at least one evening each week in rehearsal or preparation. Obviously there will be times when these commitments cannot be kept, but the effectiveness of the ministry depends on reasonable regularity. Those who have so many other responsibilities in the church that they cannot make and keep these commitments with reasonable regularity should not become team members. Instead, they might be guests of the team and serve as they are able.

ALTERNATIVE MINISTRIES

Since versatility is a mark of bridge building, the team should be open to forms of ministry other than making visits in a home, or hosting guests in your home or in a restaurant. Following are some suggestions:

1) Door-to-door canvassing

The team may lead or join the church in a community canvass, going door to door with literature and an invitation to church. Remember that opportunities for some bridge building may come in the few minutes spent at someone's doorstep.

2) Immediate contacts

The effectiveness of a contact with a visitor to the church is usually determined by how quickly it is made after the visitor has first attended church. With this in mind, get the names and telephone numbers of any first-time visitors immediately after the church service, and have someone phone them Sunday afternoon. This phone call must be brief so as not to interrupt a Sunday meal, and it should merely extend a welcome and open the way for further contacts.

3) Three-way bridge building

Visit one family and build a bridge of care. Then go with one or more members of this family to visit another family.

4) Cross-generational bridge building

Build a bridge to two or three Christian high-school students and go with them to visit some other high-school students.

5) Cross-cultural bridge building

We fare best with unfamiliar cultures when we come as humble listeners and learners. Most of our difficulties with other cultures are encountered while we are speaking and taking the upper place, but true humility, respect, and courtesy are acceptable in all cultures. Therefore, the principles of bridge building are particularly adaptable to contacts with other cultures.

6) A telephone ministry

In some communities there are resources for learning to use the telephone effectively. Combine what you learn from any such resources with your bridge building knowledge, and use your opportunities to build bridges by telephone.

CAUTION ON USE OF TELEPHONE

Remember that the telephone has brought you, uninvited, into the home of the other person, and this can be cause for resentment. He or she might be busy and be too courteous to tell you so. Be respectful and make the conversation brief unless the other person obviously wishes to extend it. In this case, continue as long as the other person desires.

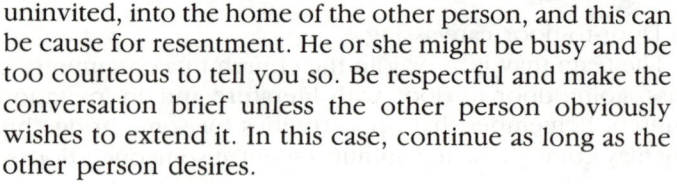

7) Building bridges to busy people

Don't skip over people because you think they may be too busy to see you. They are often lonely and need bridges built to them. Be respectful of their time, and try to make a contact at their convenience. Follow all the principles of bridge building while you are with them.

8) Assimilating new people

Bridge builders may become the personal companions or sponsors of people who are joining the church or becoming part of the fellowship. See that they are introduced to others, sit with them in church services if they desire, attend church membership classes with them, and continue to learn to care for them after they have become members.

9) Casual bridge building

Bridge building is not necessarily limited to special assignments. Review chapter three and be prepared to practice bridge building when the opportunities come.

RELATIONSHIPS WITH THE CHURCH

There should always be cooperation with the leaders of the church when a bridge building team is to be formed. The team should be accountable to some responsible administrative body, such as the diaconate.

The purpose and method of operation of the ministry should be clearly understood. There should be guidelines, but they should not be so restrictive that the team does not have the freedom to be versatile. It should be understood that the bridge building team is a working body and has no administrative authority outside itself. Its field of service should be defined so that it does not duplicate or preempt other care bodies in the church.

It will usually be best not to publicize the bridge building ministry more widely than necessary until it has become well enough established to prove itself. Any guiding rules should be of a temporary nature until the unique nature of the ministry has been determined and tested. Then these rules can be revised before being made permanent.

RELATIONSHIP WITH THE PASTOR

The team leader should keep an open relationship with the pastor. The pastor's full support will be needed if the ministry is to succeed. Pastors will benefit from this ministry because it will multiply their effectiveness. However, team members must remember that pastors have many other responsibilities and a full schedule, and should not expect more than the pastor can give.

In some small churches, the team might serve directly under the pastor, who would meet regularly with the team, and the team, in turn, would greatly enlarge the pastor's ministry. In some larger churches, the team might serve as an extension of the ministry of an associate pastor. Whatever the arrangements, the pastor and the team must cooperate closely.

INVITING PEOPLE TO BECOME CHRISTIANS

As you learn to love people, it will be natural for you to want to invite them to become Christians.

Do not become distressed if you do not feel able to do this. Turn back to page 30 and choose the alternative that is most comfortable.

The emphasis we need to keep in mind is that we are continually learning to love people. Love may lead us to some of the alternative ministries suggested elsewhere in this booklet, or it may lead us into paths that are entirely unexpected.

CHAPTER SIX

Level Three: The Team Leader

Being a team leader might well be one of the most exciting and fulfilling experiences of your life. You may be leading a group that has already been formed, or you may be recruiting and forming your own team. In either case, just imagine working with a group of Christians whose aim is to follow Jesus' example of humility, to become listeners and learners, and to concentrate on learning to love each other!

QUALIFICATIONS FOR TEAM LEADERSHIP

From the following suggested qualifications you will note that the position does not require special greatness but a willingness to humble yourself and take the place of a servant.

You should:

1) Be a committed Christian, but you should not have a need to see yourself as an outstanding Christian. So-called ordinary Christians may be better qualified.

2) Be secure enough to take the role of a servant without expecting special attention.

3) Be willing to learn, especially how to be a good listener.

4) Be willing to give this ministry first place among your responsibilities to your church. To be an effective leader you should not have other duties that will compete for the time and energy you have available.

5) Be willing to commit yourself for a significant period of time, such as one year or long enough to train someone to succeed you.

6) Be willing to assume active leadership and also to work harmoniously with other people.

7) Have a car or some other means of transportation at your disposal.

> KEEPING THE RIGHT PERSPECTIVE
> First, let us take a short break to review this ministry from the perspective of the leader:
> God's love began with the Trinity itself. Father, Son, and Holy Spirit loved one another. God's love, however, could not be contained. God created the whole universe because of his love. He created human beings, especially, so that he could love them and be loved by them in return. His love reached out, first to his own people and then to the whole world.
> The ministry of the bridge builders will follow this pattern. The loving relationships will begin within the team itself and then reach out to the people of the church and to the people outside the church. This will mean that:
> 1) As the team comes together, your first concern will be to learn to care for and build a loving relationship with-

in the team itself. This must happen before any effective bridge building can be done outside the team.

2) As you continue, this loving concern will begin reaching out to others, both within the church and outside.

Make prayer an important part of your planning and work. Since you are seeking God's perspective, it is important to keep an open line of communication with him.

GETTING STARTED

1) Become familiar with the bridge building principles outlined in the preceding chapters of this booklet. Put them into practice yourself, joining with any others who are beginning with you.

2) Revise these principles to fit your situation. You may require something quite different. Keep experimenting and revising as you go.

3) If you are recruiting your own team, begin by doing some bridge building yourself. Then invite those you are contacting, and who have the time to give, to join you in beginning this ministry. Don't be afraid of unlikely prospects. Learn to care for them and see how they respond.

4) Don't require prospective team members to accept or reject immediately. Urge them to take time to consider. Invite them to come to team meetings and observe.

5) During your first meetings get to know and understand each other well enough to share concerns and needs. Worship together. Study and discuss the bridge building principles and begin to revise them to fit your situation. Make lists of people to whom you might build bridges, like those suggested on page 33. Be sure to include a broad cross section of people.

6) Have a party or plan a retreat. Your relationships should not just revolve around work. Being together should be fun.

7) While you are getting to know one another, the team members may practice some bridge building on their own—at work,

in school, at social gatherings. Report on these experiences.

8) Go over your lists yourself or with another team member who may be willing to be responsible for keeping records.

9) Hand out assignments, several to each person, but expect only one contact each week. Begin with people who will likely be more affirming and less threatening. Don't limit yourself to people who seem to have needs. *Remember that your immediate goal is to learn to love people.*

10) Continue meetings with weekly assignments. Don't press those who feel shy. Let them hear from other team members for a few sessions.

Always keep the questions before the group: "Are you becoming a more caring person? Are you learning to care for this family or that individual? Are you learning to understand people better?" If you and your team members are becoming more understanding and more caring, other good results will be inevitable.

THE AGENDA

BASIC AGENDA

1) Time for sharing personal needs and concerns, mutual support, expressions of care, encouragement, and prayer

2) Selected reports on weekly contacts and suggestions for follow up

3) Assignments for next week

SPECIAL AGENDA ITEMS:

1) Training through Bible study, dramatization, role play, etc.

2) Responding to changing needs

3) Welcoming guests

4) Assimilating new members into the church fellowship

5) Planning special projects and dealing with special problems

6) Planning some fun and recreational activity for the team

Don't be tempted to get some minor matters out of the way at the beginning of the meeting. Use this time for priority activities.

THE SERVANT LEADER

As the leader, you will be the servant of the team. You will constantly be learning to love the team members. In learning to love them, you will be a model to them, and they will learn to love others. *If your team becomes large, you may be justified in giving your full attention to the team members, listening to them, sharing with them, and accompanying them at times as they make their contacts.*

The servant role is to be more relaxing than domineering. "You will find rest for your souls," Jesus said, "For my yoke is easy and my burden is light" (Matthew 11:29-30). You are his servant as well as the servant of the team. If things do not work out as you had hoped, you may be sure he will show you some better way.

As you assume the responsibility of ministering to the team, be sure to allow the team to minister to you. Your authority over the team does not consist in being above the team but in taking the lower place. You are in leadership, but you recognize that you are a servant whose authority has been delegated to you.

The relationships that develop within the team and between the leader and the team have the possibility of becoming the richest and most satisfying that can be found anywhere.

MAINTAINING COMMITMENT AND DISCIPLINE

Accept the fact that some team members will be less responsible than others. If the irresponsibility threatens the morale of the team, however, something should be done about it. Never reprimand or criticize a team member in the presence of others. Arrange to meet this person alone.

Don't meet with the problem person to reprimand. Rather,

meet to learn to understand and care more for him or her. As you learn more about the situation you will understand the reasons and can deal sympathetically with this person.

Perhaps he or she has too many other responsibilities or other interests and should take a leave, or there may be problems that need sympathetic understanding. This is what bridge building is all about. The other person is responding as you listen and learn.

RELATIONSHIPS WITH PASTOR AND CHURCH LEADERS

Keep in close touch with the pastor and lay leaders of the church. We always come back to the same principles—be respectful, take the lower place, and be a listener and a learner in these relationships also. You can depend on bridge building. It will work where nothing else will.

UNITE YOUR MEETINGS AND YOUR ASSIGNMENTS

The meetings and the assignments are one. Neither can exist without the other. Your assignments will provide experiences to enrich your meetings. Your meetings will provide resources for your assignments.

DRAMATIZE
At some of your meetings, dramatize one or more of the actual situations you have faced on your assignments. Have different team members play the role of different people. Try different ways to build bridges in different situations. It is fun, and a good way to learn.

REVISE
Your experiences during your assignments may teach you that the ministry is not being conducted in the most effective way. A meeting every week gives the team the opportunity to make revisions that will improve its effectiveness.

REVITALIZE

Allow the Holy Spirit to work both through the meetings and the assignments to refresh and revitalize your spiritual life. Your team will become a "nerve center" for the entire church, spreading a contagious caring spirit through the congregation.

THE GENTLE ARMY

We bridge builders are the shock troops of a gentle army. We break down barriers and build bridges between people, but we do it by persistent, quiet caring.

The Master Bridge Builder, who we follow, broke down all barriers to God and brought people who previously had been isolated from each other into loving relationships, but he did it:

1) by the Spirit

2) without force or coercion

3) so gently that he did not break the tenderest twig or quench the tiniest smoldering flame (see Matthew 12:18-20).

It is indeed remarkable that this gentle force is available, not to the great and the prestigious, but to those who are generally considered ordinary Christians.

So we go out to listen and to learn and thus to break down barriers and build bridges between people.

If there is any formula for success, it is written in Philippians 2:5: "Your attitude should be the same as that of Christ Jesus."

RESOURCES FOR SHARING THE GOSPEL

"How to Become a Christian," Wesley W. Nelson (Covenant Publications), $.15 each or $.10 for twenty or more. Available from Covenant Bookstore, 3200 West Foster Ave., Chicago, IL 60625, 800-621-1290.

"Has Anyone Ever Told You?" (Covenant Publications), $.20 each. Available from Covenant Bookstore.

Bill Bungler Learns to Visit (Church Growth and Evangelism). Bill bungles his way through six tedious visits and finally learns to visit. Thirty minute audio casette, $2.50. Available from Covenant Resource Center, 5101 North Francisco Avenue, Chicago, IL 60625, 800-338-IDEA.

What You Should Know about Sharing Your Faith (Channing L. Bete Company, Inc.), $.50. Available through Covenant Resource Center.

Becoming a Christian and ***Being a Christian,*** John R. Stott (InterVarsity Press), $.75 each.

How to Give Away Your Faith, with study guide, Paul E. Little (InterVarsity Press), $6.95, accompanying cassette $14.95. Available from Covenant Bookstore.

Prices subject to change.